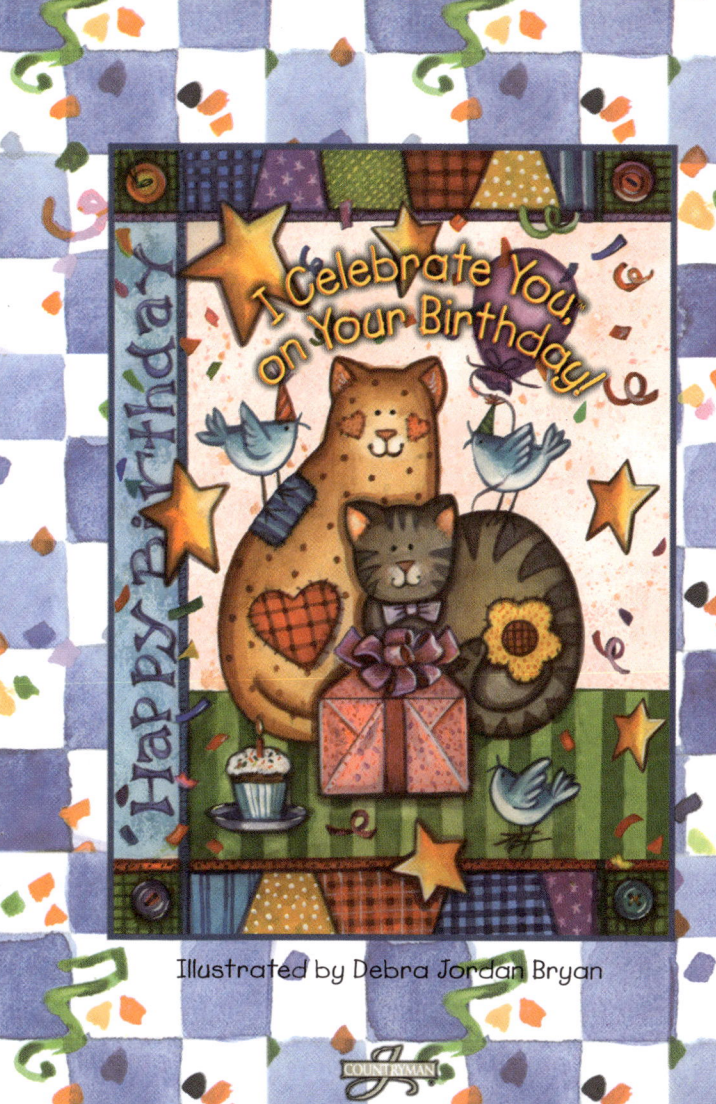

Illustrated by Debra Jordan Bryan

Copyright of illustrations 2001 by Debra Jordan Bryan

Published by J. Countryman
A division of Thomas Nelson, Inc.,
Nashville, Tennessee 37214

Project Editor—Terri Gibbs

All rights reserved.
No portion of this publication may be
reproduced, stored in a retrieval system or
transmitted in any form by any means—electronic,
mechanical, photocopying, recording, or any other—
except for brief quotations in printed reviews,
without the prior written permission of the publisher.

Designed by LeftCoast Design, Portland, Oregon

ISBN: 0-8499-9502-7

www.jcountryman.com

Printed in China

May your day
be special...
just like you!

The day you were born
is a day to celebrate.

Here is an adjective to
describe your special day!

January _____

February _____

March _____

April _____

May _____

June_____

July_____

August_____

September_____

October_____

November_____

December_____

# HAPPY

HAPPY

BIRTHDAY

You're number ONE
with me.
So hope you have
a fabulous day
that's as fun
as it can be!

BIRTHDAY

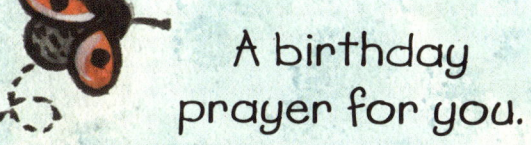

A birthday prayer for you.

_____

_____

_____

_____

_____

_____

May your special day be blessed in every way.